Original title:
Tropical Blooms

Copyright © 2025 Creative Arts Management OÜ
All rights reserved.

Author: Vivienne Beaumont
ISBN HARDBACK: 978-1-80586-384-7
ISBN PAPERBACK: 978-1-80586-856-9

The Language of Wild Orchids

In the jungle, whispers play,
Orchids giggle, come what may.
With every flap, a butterfly sighs,
And tiny ants wear funny ties.

A parrot asks, 'What's the news?'
While leafcutter ants wear fancy shoes.
Flowers gossip, all a-flutter,
'Did you see the snail's new smutter?'

Kaleidoscope in the Understory

Beneath the trees, a wild dance,
Petals twirl, if you take a chance.
Lizards break into a grand ballet,
While grasshoppers sing, 'Hip Hip Hooray!'

Frogs in bowties leap and croak,
Chasing after every joke.
Such colors shout, 'Come join the fun!'
In this haven, no need to run.

Impressions of a Blooming Haven

Sunlight spills in hues so bright,
Buzzing bees take to flight.
Chasing shadows, petals wink,
'Is that a flower, or just a pink?'

A monkey swings with cheeky glee,
Monkeys Yelp, 'Hey, look at me!'
Yellow blooms with laughter spread,
While laughing fruits roll off the bed.

The Scent of a Thousand Suns

The air is sweet, it lifts our mood,
As flowers dance, they speak of food.
But wait—was that a cheeky cat?
Chasing birds while wearing a hat?

'Life's a party!' the blooms proclaim,
'Let's mix the colors, play the game!'
With smiles bright, they stand so tall,
In this fiesta, we shall all ball.

Harmony in Bloom

In the garden, petals dance,
A bee gets lost in a bright romance.
Flowers giggle in the warm breeze,
Winking at bees, saying, "Chop chop, please!"

Colorful birds join the joyful spree,
Singing silly songs in perfect glee.
Laughter erupts from the fragrant patch,
As butterflies twirl in a lovely match.

Creations of Light and Shade

A monkey swings, holding a berry,
Laughing at the shadow of a big scary.
Lemons and limes wear hats of bright green,
Swaying to rhythms, a fruity scene.

Sunlight tickles the leaves on top,
While roots below play hopscotch and hop.
The palm trees peek with a cheeky grin,
Waiting for the next fruity win.

Jewels of the Sunlit Path

Walking down the path, oh what a sight,
Glimmers of color burst left and right.
Daisies act like they're in a parade,
With bumbles and wiggles, they're not afraid.

A lizard prances on a leaf or two,
Daring the ants to come join the view.
The sun smiles down with a twinkling ray,
As daisies giggle, just another day.

Awakening of the Canopy

In the canopy's arms, a coo-coo cries,
While parrots argue about the prize.
The trunks blush with stories untold,
As squirrels race in a contest bold.

Leaves whisper secrets to the dancing air,
While mischief brews everywhere.
Jungle gym for critters and fun,
With laughter echoing under the sun!

Flourishing in Harmony

In a garden where laughter grows,
Flowers dance in silly clothes.
Petals giggle in the breeze,
Bouncing round like bumblebees.

Sunshine serves a double dose,
Painting cheeks of blushing rose.
Even weeds are dressed with flair,
Dancing under sunny glare.

Bees perform their buzzing tune,
While frogs take turns to croon.
Who knew blooms could play so nice?
Their antics surely do entice!

Laughter spills with every bloom,
Filling every corner, room.
In this patch of mirth and cheer,
Nature's jokes are crystal clear.

Garden of Whimsy

Welcome to the giggling glade,
Where the daffodils have played.
With butterflies in silly hats,
And squirrels chatting with the bats.

Daisies wave their tiny hands,
Cheering for their flower bands.
While tulips attempt to jive,
With moves that barely stay alive.

The sunflowers are acting bold,
Strutting like they own the gold.
While the violets share a jest,
Claiming they're the garden's zest.

This garden's filled with dreams so bright,
Every corner brings delight.
If you're sad, please come and see,
The blooms that joke so joyfully.

The Artistry of the Wild

In the wild where colors blend,
Monkey jokes that never end.
Petunias prance with floppy feet,
Turning mundane into a treat.

Cacti wear the spikiest ties,
And orchids toss flamboyant sighs.
Laughter bubbles, fills the air,
Every critter joins the fair.

A quiet lily starts to snore,
While daisies roll for just one score.
The jungle shakes with planty pranks,
As nature gives her playful winks.

So step inside this floral spree,
Where even trees dance with glee.
In this patch of vivid art,
Every bloom plays a funny part.

The Heartbeat of Greenery

In the jungle gym of leaves,
Lizards do the salsa, if you please.
Dancing by the ferns, they sway,
And giggle at the bees' ballet.

Such a vibrant show, they'll boast,
Caterpillars toast with their jam toast.
Every leaf a stage, it seems,
Where flowers burst like silly dreams.

Vibrations of the Wildflower

Dandelions whisper jokes with glee,
While daisies drop puns like confetti.
Sunflowers wave, they're such hams,
    Pulling faces at passing clams.

The wind's a DJ; flowers breakdance,
In grass skirt style, they take a chance.
Petals twirl in a wild parade,
    While butterflies laugh and serenade.

Flowers in the Rain

Raindrops tap dance on petal tips,
Tulips don't mind, they shake their hips.
Bumblebees frown, their wigs get wet,
Crying, 'Oh no! My hair's a mess yet!'

Pansies wear puddles, a fashion tease,
While orchids giggle at soggy bees.
Laughter echoes in every drop,
As petals jiggle and never stop.

Whispers of the Canopy

Leaves gossip in the breezy air,
'Look at that squirrel, a true daredevil square!'
Monkeys chuckle, swinging high,
While parrots joke about a pie.

Lianas swing with a viney grin,
As sunbeams dance on their leafy kin.
Every branch a place to share,
Eager giggles float everywhere.

Twilight Blossoms

In the garden, blooms sway,
Dancing to a breezy play.
Monkeys giggle, flowers cheer,
Petals whisper, "Spring is here!"

Colors clash like clowns in hats,
Buzzing bees wear tiny spats.
Each bud tells a joke or pun,
Underneath the setting sun.

Dandelions wear sunglasses bright,
As fireflies come out at night.
Laughter echoes, scents collide,
In this garden, joy won't hide.

The Magic of the Mangrove

Down by the roots, crabs have a dance,
Wiggling around, giving fate a chance.
Seagulls crack jokes in the salty breeze,
While fish gossip about island teas.

The trees hold secrets, play card games,
With lizards in suits, what are their names?
Each branch a stage, each wave a cheer,
In the mangrove theater, laughter's near.

A pelican strolls, a hat on his beak,
Winking at tourists who come to sneak.
With every quirk, the shore comes alive,
In this watery world, joy will thrive.

Waves of Vibrant Life

Surfboards sprout like daisies bright,
Riding on waves with pure delight.
Starfish giggle, wearing cool shades,
Life under water never fades.

Anemones wave like they're at a ball,
While clowns in coral make fun of it all.
Dolphins leap high, a comical sight,
To splash the beach with sheer delight.

Crabby parties, what a riot,
Seashells join in, oh, what a sight!
In the ocean's giggle, every wave's a song,
Bouncing with joy, nothing feels wrong.

Hues of the Island

Sunset paints the sky in glee,
With colors that dance, wild and free.
Bananas wear hats and laugh out loud,
While coconuts gather in a crowd.

Parrots squawk in a vibrant choir,
Verses of humor that never tire.
Each flower poses with a wink,
A floral fashion show, don't you think?

An island sweet shop, treats galore,
Lollipops giggle, yearning for more.
Breezes carry funny tales untold,
In this world of color, warmth unfolds.

The Pulse of Flora at Dusk

In the garden, petals twirl,
Dancing softly, a floral whirl.
Bees wear top hats, buzzing with flair,
While crickets play jazz without a care.

Fireflies flicker, a light show spree,
Chatting with leaves, quite the jubilee.
Nature's party, with laughter and glee,
All join the festivity, wild and free.

Whirlwind of Color in the Rainforest

Vines are giggling, swinging about,
Parrots join, with a colorful shout.
Monkeys in hats swing by with delight,
As flowers blow kisses, oh what a sight!

A chameleon winks, changes his hue,
While frogs play leapfrog, what a rendezvous!
Nature's paint palette flings color galore,
In this vibrant jungle, we simply want more.

Whispers of the Hibiscus

A hibiscus wearing a floppy wide brim,
Whispers sweet secrets, dreams on a whim.
Its petals like laughter, bright and loud,
Enticing the clouds to float and be proud.

With each gentle sway, stories unfold,
Of bees in tuxedos, oh so bold.
Frogs with their croaks join in the jest,
In the laughter of blooms, we feel so blessed.

Dance of the Frangipani

Frangipanis pirouette under the moon,
They sway to the rhythm of a soft tune.
Bamboo sticks tap, like a conga line,
While sleeping bats dream of grapes on the vine.

A breeze takes a spin, skirts made of green,
And butterflies flutter, looking quite keen.
With blooms breaking out in cheeky ballet,
The night bursts with joy, come join the display!

Secrets in the Orchid's Heart

Oh, did you see that funky orchid?
It wears a hat, goes out and dances.
With polka dots and a twisty stem,
It dreams of being in a flower trance.

Bumblebees gossip, sipping tea,
They say the rose is quite the flirt.
While daisies plan their next big move,
Sunflowers just bask, as if they're alert.

Orchids hide secrets in petal folds,
Whispers of trivia they barely glean.
Like, who really snuck into the garden?
To steal a cup from the lavender team!

The nightingale sings, but who can tell?
If that was a tune or squawking noise?
The flowers giggle, petals aflutter,
In this garden, it's all about poise.

Sunlit Petals

In my garden, under sunny gaze,
Daisies play hopscotch, laze away.
One said, 'I'll catch some rays today!'
While others giggle, 'Come what may!'

Petunias wear shades, looking quite cool,
While others gossip about the old rule.
They say sun will make you shout with glee,
But too much and you may lose your spree.

A lily spreads rumors, oh so grand,
Of a sunflower's dance that's unplanned.
But the violets chuckle, sly and sweet,
While plotting ways to stomp on defeat.

So remember this on a bright sunny day,
In flower talk, it's all just play.
With each petal that flutters, you'll see it too,
Life's a garden, meant for a joyful view!

Garden of Lush Colors

Welcome to the color blast, my friend,
Where every flower has a tale to send.
Roses blushing, they just can't hide,
Their secrets of love, like a garden ride.

Hibiscus flaunts, in vibrant glory,
Tells tales of wind, oh what a story!
While marigolds nod, in the warm breeze,
Setting the stage for chuckles with ease.

With every bloom, there's a teaser or two,
A daffodil boasting that it's all true.
'Watch out!' yells the tulip, as it plays a trick,
'Next time you sneeze, don't blame the pollen thick!'

In this masterpiece, colors collide,
Nature's laughter, a joyous tide.
So come join in, let the petals swirl,
In this garden prank, where fun does twirl!

Serenade of the Bougainvillea

Oh, Bougainvillea, you're quite the tease,
With your purple crown blowing in the breeze.
Neighbors stare as you show off your flair,
While all the other plants just stop and stare.

You swayed in the wind, like a hip-hop star,
And the palm trees roll their eyes from afar.
They say you're too bold, a real show-off,
But look at them, trying hard not to scoff!

Your petals whisper secrets in the heat,
'Bet I can catch that bee on one sweet cheat!'
While the fern laughs low, 'Oh what a game!'
In this laughable bloom, it's never the same.

So here's to the colors that dance all around,
Where laughter and petals together are found.
In this serenade, it's clear as can be,
Life's just a joke; come giggle with me!

The Secret Life of Blooms

In the garden, petals dance,
Wiggling 'round like they've got plans.
Underneath the moon's big eye,
They gossip just like you and I.

Bumbling bees buzz with a grin,
Sneaking nectar, their daily sin.
When the sun creeps high in the sky,
They pretend they're just passing by.

Daisies throw a wild party,
Crack jokes with the dandelions, hearty.
While orchids boast of colorful flair,
Their shyness? Just a clever scare.

Roses pucker, oh how they pout,
Kissing the air without a doubt.
With laughter, they share their sweet perfume,
In a world where joy will always bloom.

Radiance on the Water's Edge

Lilies float like boats in a race,
Trying to win the water's embrace.
They giggle when the ripples tease,
Making waves, oh what a breeze!

Sunflowers turn with the sun's smile,
Practicing poses, going for style.
While the turtles glance with delight,
At blooms dazzling in sunlight.

Frogs croak their own kind of song,
Bouncing on pads where they belong.
With petals winking, bright and bold,
Nature's jesters, never too old.

Every splash brings joy and cheer,
As flowers sway, they shed a tear.
But don't be fooled by their gentle sway,
They're plotting mischief, come what may.

Enigma in the Garden

Petals whisper, secrets untold,
In a world where mysteries unfold.
Why do daisies wear such a crown?
It's said they're the quirkiest around.

Marigolds giggle in golden tones,
Playing hide and seek with garden gnomes.
At dusk, they prank the neighboring weeds,
Tickle their roots, plant funny seeds.

The hibiscus dons a bright, loud coat,
Singing songs that make flowers gloat.
While vines sneak in, stretching out wide,
Hoping to hitch a fun, goofy ride.

So wander here, where laughter flows,
Among the blooms, anything goes.
Each petal, a clue in life's game,
Where silliness is the sweetest claim.

Burst of Color

In the meadow, hues collide,
Bright reds, yellows, a joyful slide.
Petunias grab the sun's warm rays,
While busy bees drone in a daze.

Pink flamingos strut with flair,
Judging blooms with a sassy stare.
Who can blame them? They love to boast,
In this lively garden, they're the host.

Forget-me-nots wink, "Oh, do stay!"
Inviting all for a colorful play.
With every shade, a vibrant cheer,
Life's a canvas; come join the sphere!

So laugh with me as colors blend,
Let's twirl our petals 'til the end.
In this burst, we find our tune,
Where funny blossoms always bloom.

The Solstice Bloom

In a garden where coconuts play,
The flowers giggle and sway all day.
A parrot sings a silly tune,
While daisies dance under the moon.

The sunflowers gossip, full of cheer,
Saying, 'Look at my height, I'm better, my dear!'
A rose blushes, feeling quite grand,
Wishing she could be part of a band.

Flamingos prance, wearing pink shades,
Making the bees do some funny charades.
With every bloom, there's laughter and fun,
In this paradise where jokes weigh a ton.

But wait, what's that? A gardener shouts,
'Pick the flowers, what are you about?'
They scatter and laugh, not wanting to go,
In their vibrant world, the fun's all aglow.

Vibrant Fables of Flora

In a tale where petals wear shoes,
The lilies play cards, sharing their news.
A cactus juggles tiny green balls,
While violets tell tales that bring hearty chuckles.

The daisies burst out with laughter so bright,
Telling stories of bees that take flight.
"Oh dear, they drank nectar, fell off their chairs,
Now buzzing in circles, they've forgotten their cares!"

A giant rose claims she's queen of the plot,
With a crown made of leaves, she says she's so hot.
The ferns roll their eyes, whispering in jest,
"We know where you hide all your thorns, yes!"

As the sun sets, the garden's a sight,
With fireflies flickering, making it bright.
The blooms may be silly, but they truly know,
That life's just a romp, where laughter will grow.

The Enchanted Grove

In a grove where giggles run free,
The fruit trees wear hats, just wait and see.
Papayas discuss the weather so grand,
While bananas befriend a tree-climbing band.

Tall palms wave hello with a breeze,
Tickled by whispers of buzzing bees.
"Did you hear," quipped a cheeky old trunk,
"Our flowers secretly dance when the sun's sunk!"

Beneath the shade, a pickle-shaped vine,
Sings to the crowd, "Come on now, be fine!"
The mushrooms chuckle, all spry and quick,
Watching the blossoms do their silly tricks.

But soon a blunder, a squirrel runs fast,
With acorns in tow, he trips and falls flat.
Yet laughter erupts, echoing so wide,
As the grove comes alive, bursting with pride.

Blossoms of Joy

In a meadow where laughter grows tall,
The tulips tell jokes, giving their all.
A tiny orchid wears a proud frown,
Saying, "Make way for the queen of this town!"

The sunbeams chuckle, tickling the grass,
While marigolds wink, as bright as glass.
"Did you hear," said a daisy with flair,
"Fat honeybees can't dance, not a care!"

A petunia tries to bust a fine move,
But stumbles and rolls, it's hard to improve.
The daisies all giggle as she begins,
To wriggle and shake, as laughter ensues.

At the end of the day, the blooms all unite,
With petals flapping, what a funny sight!
In this garden, where whimsies deploy,
Life blossoms sweetly, spreading pure joy.

The Art of Flourishing

In a garden where laughter grows,
Petals giggle and bend like foes.
Sunshine dances on leaves so bright,
Bees buzz by in sheer delight.

Worms in shades of purple and green,
Sneakily munch on leaves, unseen.
The daisies wear hats, quite the sight,
While roses gossip into the night.

Cacti claim they're the toughest crowd,
While orchids pose, divinely proud.
A butterfly winks from up high,
Sipping nectar, flying by.

In this art where colors clash,
Find laughter hidden in every splash.
A bloom that trips, a vine that slips,
In this joyful space, friendship grips.

In the Shade of Fronds

Under the palms where the shadows play,
Lizards dance without a say.
Coconut fell with a thud so loud,
A squirrel fled, joining the crowd.

Bright parrots squawk with flair so bold,
Sharing secrets that never grow old.
While ferns giggle and sway in the breeze,
Collapsing under their own cheeky tease.

Suddenly, a monkey swings by,
Wearing a hat made of pie, oh my!
He offers a slice to a rose in bloom,
Who just giggles and fills up the room.

In this shade, a party convenes,
With punch served in pineapples, it seems.
A melody of colors, nothing is bland,
Here in the fronds, life's simply grand.

Portraits of Eden

Let's hang up some portraits, they say,
Of blossoms that dance in the sun's display.
A sunflower strikes quite a pose,
While lilacs blush in a soft repose.

Daisies giggle in neat little rows,
Bragging about their fashion shows.
Tulips flaunt colors, oh so bright,
Under the sparkle of morning light.

A bumblebee hums with a comic flair,
Buzzing artfully without a care.
"What's this?" it asks, in a tone so sly,
A petunia with sunglasses nearby!

So, hang them up, these vivid sights,
In the gallery of laughter and lights.
Where blooms share giggles and sneaky winks,
Creating joy more than one thinks.

Violets in the Emerald Haze

Violets twirl in emerald grass,
Claiming the title of sassy class.
Dancing 'round, they draw the eye,
With petals laughing, saying hi!

The daisies join in with a shout,
"Who's the fairest?" they dance about.
The violets giggle, full of glee,
"Let's just bloom and be merry, like we!"

In the haze where colors spin,
Bees partake in the joyous din.
A ladybug winks and says, "Oh please,
Let's have a party with branches and leaves!"

Under the sun, the humor flows,
In vibrant hues where happiness grows.
Violets whisper sweet escapades,
In this lush land, joy never fades.

Sun-Kissed Petals

In gardens where the sun does cheer,
Flowers burst forth, oh so near.
They giggle as they sway with grace,
Waving at bees, a dancing race.

Petals plop like jellybeans,
Wobbling in their sunny jeans.
One flower tries to do a flip,
Ends up giggling, a comical trip.

With colors bright, they paint the town,
A floral circus, never a frown.
They hold a party, very neat,
Inviting ants to move their feet.

So here's to blooms, both bold and bright,
They bring us joy, pure delight!
In their silly, sunlit dance,
Life's a garden, take a chance!

A Language of Blooms

In every petal, secrets hide,
Whispering stories far and wide.
A daisy said, "Oh, take a look!"
While marigolds wrote a funny book.

Roses giggle in shades of red,
With jokers hiding underbed.
Tulips quip, "We're very grand!"
Chilling out, in the flower band.

Lilies flaunt their polka dots,
Making fun of the snobby pots.
Sunflowers yell, "We're number one!"
Chasing bugs just for fun!

So let's decipher this quirky lore,
Amongst the blooms, there's always more.
With laughter brewed in every shade,
A garden party, no need to trade!

The Veil of Color

A splash of pink, a dash of blue,
These blooms can really play it true.
Dressed in colors, oh so bright,
They giggle softly in the light.

Pansies wear a jester's cap,
Sitting low, they take a nap.
Dahlias bloom with a funny face,
Chasing shadows in a race.

Petunias shout, "Can you hear me?!"
In this flower dance, so carefree.
They twirl in breezes, oh what fun,
Each one joins in, a blooming run!

A riot of hues, the petals play,
Drawing laughter day by day.
In this garden, joy abounds,
Where every sprout brings silly sounds!

Fragrant Whispers at Dusk

As evening falls, the scents arise,
With giggles shared beneath the skies.
Jasmine whispers, "Play a tune,"
While violets dance beneath the moon.

Hibiscus blushes, quite the show,
Saying, "Watch me steal the glow!"
Lavender winks, and so does thyme,
Making fragrance a funny rhyme.

Orchids prance in posh attire,
Daring others to join the choir.
They boast, "We bloom like superstars!"
Twinkling bright, like evening jars.

So gather 'round, let's share a laugh,
Under blooms, we'll carve our path.
With scented whispers, life's a kick,
In fragrant fun, let's make it stick!

A Symphony of Blossoms

The daisies dance, quite a sight,
As kookaburras take to flight.
Lillies shout, 'Stop smelling me!'
While sunflowers grin with glee.

The ferns wear hats, so bright and round,
While cacti hope to not fall down.
They chuckle loud at passing bees,
Who buzz by quickly, if you please.

Roses gossip, what a show,
'Look at that tulip, how it glows!'
Violets joke about the rain,
While orchids sashay on the lane.

A garden band of crazy hues,
With every bloom spreading the news.
Nature's jesters, oh what a thrill,
In this colorful floral hill.

Dreams Beneath the Palms

Underneath the leafy sway,
Cockatoos plan a play.
They squawk and screech with wild delight,
While lizards bask in morning light.

A monkey swings with all its grace,
And sloths just laugh, 'We need more space!'
Coconuts drop, oh what a game,
As parrots shout, 'Now that's no shame!'

The hibiscus blushes red and bold,
'I'm the star! Watch stories unfold!'
But palm fronds roll their eyes in jest,
'You're just a flower, we're the best!'

With dreams wrapped in sunshine rays,
The island laughs through endless days.
Every bloom, a tale to weave,
In this paradise, we believe.

Echoes of the Passionflower

Passionflowers mockingly spin,
'Come for a drink, just let us in!'
They giggle soft, their colors bright,
'The bees are here, what a delight!'

'The lovesick vines creep up so fast,
While butterflies flit, oh such a blast!'
Petals whisper to the breeze,
'Verse your thoughts, have fun with ease!'

In this jungle, jokes abound,
As monkeys bounce around the ground.
They tease the flowers, playfully taunt,
'Your perfume's strong; it's not a haunt!'

Echoes laughing through the leaves,
Nature smiles, a touch of thieves.
Spreading joy, a wondrous flair,
In every bloom, there's laughter to share.

Palette of the Paradise

In the palette of this land,
Colors meet, quite unplanned.
Mixing hues like paint on skin,
Watch the flowers spin and grin!

Golden yellows, reds so hot,
Together they form quite a lot.
They pester bees, just for fun,
Playing tag 'til day is done.

'Hey you, come try our perfume sip!
It's way better than your trip!'
Tulips cheer, 'We're the chosen few!'
While begonias say, 'We'll join too!'

In this scene of vivid cheer,
Every petal has a sneer.
A palette bright that sings with glee,
Nature's jesters, wild and free.

A Canopy of Color

Vines hang low with bright delight,
Chasing butterflies in flight.
Leaves wear hues, a vibrant show,
Dancing in the breeze, oh so slow.

In this jungle, I must roam,
Finding flowers far from home.
A parrot squawks, a monkey grins,
Play hide and seek, that's where it begins.

Petals dropping like a tease,
Nature's way to say "Oh please!"
Sunlight giggles through the trees,
Tickling noses with a breeze.

Throw caution to the vibrant air,
In this chaos, laughter's there.
Color splashes all around,
In this jungle, joy is found.

Flora's Gentle Embrace

Certain blooms just love to hug,
Wrapping leaves like a warm mug.
Plants can dance without a care,
In this garden, joy is rare.

Petal parties in the sun,
Bees show up to have some fun.
Bumblebees with fuzzy coats,
Buzzing tunes and funny quotes.

Sun drops down, what a sight!
Pollen madness feels so right.
Sneezes echo, laughter flies,
Amidst colors that surprise.

Watch out for that clumsy vine,
Always tripping, oh so fine.
Flora's giggles, can't escape,
In this garden, joy takes shape.

Petals on the Wind

Petals swirling like a dream,
Twirling, whirling, like a scream.
In a breeze they whirl about,
Nature's dance without a doubt.

Here comes a butterfly in style,
Flapping by with a cheeky smile.
Roses blush, and daisies wave,
In this garden, fun we crave.

Silly squirrels join the show,
Chasing flowers to and fro.
Laughter echoes in bright tones,
As petals play among the stones.

Let the winds take us away,
Where flowers laugh and children play.
Upside down and sideways too,
In this chaos, joy is true.

Lush Reveries

A jungle gym in dazzling hues,
Where even shadows sing the blues.
Sloths hang out in slow motion,
Mixing laughter with the ocean.

Fragrant blooms in wild array,
Making every dull day sway.
Colors giggle, scents have fun,
Nature's party has begun.

Lemonade trees and cherry pies,
Caterpillars wearing ties.
A babbling brook sings a tune,
As flowers bloom beneath the moon.

Wrap me up in laughter's cloak,
As funny blooms begin to poke.
In this haven, joy's supreme,
Living bright, a vibrant dream.

Nectar and Nightfall

In the jungle, bugs convene,
Sipping nectar like it's caffeine.
Flowers dance in the moon's light,
Bees giggle, oh what a sight!

Lemurs swing in disco flair,
Wearing petals in their hair.
They twirl and spin with such grace,
Chasing shadows in this space.

The frogs croak a silly tune,
Underneath a wobbly moon.
With each hop, they ignite a laugh,
Nature's party, what a path!

So join the feast, sip the night,
Bugs in black-tie, what a sight!
With every bloom, a silly cheer,
In this garden, joy is near!

The Rise of the Plumeria

Plumeria blooms, a sight to see,
With colors that shout, 'Look at me!'
They wear a crown, oh so bright,
Competing with stars in the night.

A bee stumbles, laughs in flight,
Bumping petals left and right.
"Excuse me! I'm just passing through,"
"Didn't see that! How are you?"

The blossoms giggle, sway and poke,
Tickled by every passing joke.
They whisper secrets to the breeze,
While lizards join with wobbly knees.

A flower brawl breaks out, it seems,
To see who's the star of dream-filled themes.
But in the end it's plain to see,
Together they bloom in jubilee!

Aroma from the Canopy

The canopy holds a fragrant treat,
Banana bread—well, not quite sweet.
But as you waft through leafy trails,
You're tempted to follow scent-filled tales.

A parrot squawks, "Not my fault!"
As he munches on a tropical vault.
Laughter echoes from the trees,
As monkeys tease with playful ease.

Pineapple bursts from every nook,
While squirrels put on a cooking book.
In the air, a hodgepodge whirls,
Channeling all the snack-time girls.

Nature's buffet is quite the feast,
Where every fruit is a jesting beast.
Come, join the fun, no need to roam,
In this fragrant world, you're home!

Secrets in the Scented Breeze

Whispers float on the scented air,
As flowers share secrets without a care.
"Did you see that bee misstep?"
"He laughed so hard, he lost his pep!"

Curly vines twist, giggling low,
They hide behind blooms in a glow.
"Who will bloom first? What's the stake?"
"I know a joke that'll make him shake!"

Scented breezes play hide and seek,
Pulling pranks, just for the week.
"Hey! Watch the petals; they're not shy!"
"Tell them jokes, let's aim for the sky!"

So let's share laughter, let joy sway,
In this garden where blooms play.
With every sniff and every tease,
Life's a party in the scented breeze!

Fragrant Tales of the Wild

In a jungle full of chatter,
The flowers fight for the crown,
With petals bright, they prance about,
Like clowns in a flowery gown.

Lemons dance with the hibiscus,
While daisies play hopscotch all day,
A rose told a joke, a laugh erupted,
Even thorns had a part in the play.

Sunflowers, they cheer, quite a sight,
As bees buzz along with delight,
Pollen parties on every stem,
Who knew plants could live so spry and bright?

So grab your hat and join the fun,
In this garden where laughter's spun,
Each bloom has a tale, a laugh, a cheer,
In the wild, where silliness is number one!

Where Colors Meet the Sky

Colors collide in a garden plot,
Yellow tulips have a sunbeam fight,
The violets giggle, with laughter caught,
While clouds of cotton candy take flight.

Red petals whisper of secrets bold,
Chasing the breeze, they outshine the sun,
The bluebells cheer as the stories unfold,
In this caper of petals, everyone's won!

Orchids wear glasses, looking so wise,
Watching the sun roll down from above,
While a dandelion, with a fluttering sigh,
Sends wishes to stars, all sprinkled with love.

At the twilight party the shadows blend,
Balloons made of blooms start to ascend,
In this vibrant place, with a giggle or two,
Where colors and laughter simply won't end!

Blossoms Beneath the Moonlight

Under the moon, the flora prance,
A moonflower whispers a late-night tune,
Jasmine twirls, caught in a dance,
While night-blooming cacti swoon.

Laughter echoes from petals clad,
The marigolds tell tales of the day,
As the other blooms giggle and pad,
Under the stars, they frolic and sway.

"Why did the seed cross the road?" they tease,
To reach the light and join the fun!
With rosy cheeks and a wink, they please,
Moonlit mischief has only begun!

Beneath constellations, there's no goodbye,
Just relentless joy as the night drifts by,
In this garden of laughs, forever in sight,
Where blooms bloom brightly in shimmering light.

Kiss of the Morning Dew

Morning breaks with a fresh, cool kiss,
As dewdrops giggle on petals bright,
They dance around, who could resist?
Nature's laughter, a pure delight.

The daisies wiggle in the playful breeze,
Winking at sunflowers, oh what a tease!
"Let's play hide and seek," they say with glee,
As butterflies flutter and chirps fill the trees.

A bright bloom claims "I'm the silliest here,"
As bees buzz in, no need to steer,
With laughter in petals, they spin round and round,
In the morning's embrace, joy is found.

When the sun rises high, and the dew starts to fade,
The blooms will remember the fun that they made,
From whispers to laughter, their stories accrue,
In a world full of wonders, kissed by the dew!

Blooming in the Heart of Eden

In the garden where the fruits all dance,
The pineapples wear a party prance.
Coconuts wobble, all dressed in glee,
While guavas sing songs of the sea.

A flamingo slipped on a mango's skin,
With a honk and a flap, let the fun begin!
The orchids chuckle in vibrant hue,
As the banana leaves giggle, 'Oh, look at you!'

Bumblebees buzz with a comedic flair,
Trying to juggle the pollen mid-air.
While papayas gossip with skins so bright,
Their laughter echoes from morning till night.

In Eden's heart, joy floats like a kite,
With flowers that can make the dullest day bright.
So join the fiesta, don't be a bore,
In this garden of giggles, come dance on the floor!

Laughter of the Rainforest Flowers

In the jungle where the colors collide,
The hibiscus winks, taking pride.
A frangipani fell for a tree,
And now they're the talk of the bee.

The ferns wear hats made of mossy lace,
While squirrels race in a flowered chase.
A toucan jokes with a parrot's grin,
Together they chuckle, let the fun begin!

Dandelions dance as a breeze takes its chance,
Swaying around in a comical trance.
The lilies mimic the pond's gentle sway,
As frogs croak jokes, "It's a flower buffet!"

In this green world, smiles bloom so bright,
With chortles and giggles, it's pure delight.
So grab your basket, let the laughter pour,
As we feast on the humor this jungle has in store!

Petal-painting the Sky

Petals in pots find a way to glide,
Colors like sprinkles from gardens wide.
Sunflowers twist in a silly ballet,
While daisies tumble in the light of the day.

A butterfly stretches, trying to flex,
With pollen-prize dreams that it hopes to annex.
The marigolds giggle, "Can you beat this?"
As every flower joins in the fun, oh bliss!

Lilies leap over sunbeams with flair,
While roses complain it's too hot to bear.
"Let's splash in the raindrops or hide in a tree,"
"Sounds like a plan, maybe we'll see a bee!"

Painting the sky with laughter so free,
A symphony of petals, pure jubilee.
With a wink and a smile, we spread cheer all around,
In this canvas of color, joy can be found!

Sunlight Through Sapphire Leaves

Beneath the bright canopy, a giggle grows,
As sunlight tickles the sapphire shows.
Leaves chatter secrets with mischief in mind,
Share whispers of blooms and each feathered find.

A bright bluebird plays tag with a bee,
While lizards sunbathe, so laid back and free.
The vines twist with laughter, a colorful mess,
As they try to impress with their leafy dress.

Gumdrop flowers tumble, bounce off the ground,
Screaming with joy, what a sight, what a sound!
Vivid and sparkling, they steal the day,
While sunbeams try hard, "No shadows, we play!"

Under this vibrant, sunlit embrace,
Nature's humor we find, never a dull space.
So let's laugh together in this leafy retreat,
With each ray of sunlight, our joy is complete!

Echoes of Eden

In a garden where the pineapples dance,
Coconuts tumble, they take their chance.
Laughter erupts from playful vines,
As sunflowers gossip and sip on wines.

Bumblebees buzz with humorous flair,
While cheeky monkeys swing without a care.
Hilarity blooms in every flower sprout,
In this Eden, joy is never in doubt.

The skies burst with colors, vibrant and bold,
Petunias chuckle as stories unfold.
Every leaf whispers a jovial tune,
Under the gaze of a mischievous moon.

Fruits wear smiles, they gleam and grin,
While ants engage in a comical spin.
In this paradise, laughter resides,
Among the blooms, where joy abides.

Fruitful Elegy

Oh, the bananas in yellow burst bright,
They slip and slide in an amusing fight.
Meanwhile, strawberries sport little hats,
Sipping lemonade with the chubby cats.

Citrus fruits giggle, they tickle the breeze,
Cacti tell jokes while embracing the tease.
Mangoes rumble in a fruity choir,
While papayas prank each other with fire.

Every bumpkin bloom is a playful sight,
With gags and tricks from morning to night.
In this fruity realm, no frowns allowed,
Just laughter echoing, merry and loud.

So let's dance in the fields, not worry and fret,
In our garden of giggles, let's not forget.
That in petals and fruits, laughter's the key,
In this fruitful elegy, just let it be.

Blooming Horizons

With hibiscus hats, the blooms take flight,
Swaying and swirling, what a silly sight!
Each petal a wink, a jest, a cheer,
As the sun tickles them, spreading the cheer.

Violets engage in a dance-off, oh my!
While daisies giggle, swaying up high.
Orchids strike poses, they know they're so grand,
Competing for laughs, the best in the land.

The horizon's aglow with twinkling glee,
Brief charades between the tall palm trees.
In a realm of blooms, not one takes a frown,
With every new joke, the world turns upside down.

So come, celebrate with petals galore,
In this blooming paradise, there's always more.
Where sunshine and laughter bloom hand in hand,
Join the fun in this whimsical land.

The Garden's Lullaby

In the garden where laughter grows wild,
The flowers sing sweetly, like a child.
Butterflies twirl, they whirl and prance,
As bumblebees hum in a joyous dance.

Napping daisies dream of jelly bean treats,
While tulips tickle the earth with their beats.
Cacti crack jokes, they're quite the delight,
Under the stars that twinkle so bright.

The night brings a lullaby, soft and bright,
As fruits tell tales in the quiet light.
With every rustle, the humor flows free,
In this garden, pure bliss is the key.

So let's celebrate the mirth and the cheer,
Among petals and laughter, there's nothing to fear.
In the garden's embrace, we drift and we sway,
With a giggle and wink, we'll dance till the day.

Chronicles of the Petal

A flower wore a silly hat,
With polka dots and stripes of spat.
It danced around the buzzing bees,
And shouted, "Bring me more of these!"

The rose proclaimed with a wink,
"I smell great, but let's not think!"
The daisies giggled, petals bright,
As they twirled in pure delight.

Lilies laughed at the sun's big grin,
"Your rays are hot; let's twist and spin!"
In the garden, joy's the trend,
With each wag, flowers would extend.

So gather 'round this floral crew,
Where petals share a joke or two.
In each bloom, a jest does hide,
In the garden, laughter's our guide.

Routes of Vibrance

A sunflower lost its way one day,
It said, "To the disco, I will sway!"
With bright yellow shoes and a funky beat,
It boogied on down to a floral street.

The hibiscus with its fiery hue,
Said, "Let's paint this town a vibrant blue!"
With petals flaring, they took a chance,
And soon spread joy with every dance.

Down the path where the colors blend,
Petal pals laughed, from start to end.
They played hopscotch with honeybees,
Whirling about, hoping for some breeze.

When nightfall came, they twinkled bright,
Beneath the stars, what a funny sight!
In this garden, cheer never tires,
With every leaf, the fun never expires.

Laughter in Bloom

In the garden where giggles sound,
A clumsy tulip tripped on the ground.
With petals flailing like a mad kite,
It chuckled, "Well, that was quite a fight!"

The orchids whispered, "Do you see?"
"What do we do with all this glee?"
With smiles so wide, they spread the cheer,
And colored the day with joy sincere.

Petunias painted jokes on their leaves,
As violets tried their best to tease.
"Why did the bud refuse to bloom?"
"In case it fell, and met its doom!"

So in the patch where laughter grows,
Every petal surely knows,
That life's a riot, come take a peek,
Here in the garden, joy's unique.

Dancing on the Rainforest Floor

In the heart of the jungle, vibes running high,
A quirky fern waved its fronds, oh my!
With a wiggle and twist, it set the beat,
And plants all around hopped to their feet.

The dancing flora cheered from below,
Twirling and swirling, putting on a show.
A vine did a shimmy, so spry and bold,
While the giant leaves giggled, never cold.

The anthuriums boogied with flair,
As butterflies joined without a care.
The gears of joy turned smoothly through,
While rain dripped down like a breezy dew.

So come join the party, don't be late,
With flora and fauna, it's simply great!
In the rain forest, we dance and play,
Where laughter blooms in a merry ballet.

Enchanted by Blossoms' Breath

In a meadow so bright and alive,
Bees dance like they're trying to jive.
The petals giggle as they sway,
Even the sun seems to play today.

With colors that tease the eye and soul,
Each flower whispers, "Come take a stroll!"
A parrot shouts, "Don't miss this sight!"
As shadows wear hues of pure delight.

Beneath the blooms, a lizard prances,
Dressed in colors, making odd glances.
With every flutter, there's laughter shared,
In nature's game, none are spared!

So sip the nectar, enjoy the cheer,
Join the festivities, don't disappear!
For in this garden, silliness reigns,
And every petal has something to gain.

Prismatic Dreams Beneath the Palms

Beneath the palms, where shadows play,
Lizards wear socks in a humorous way.
A snapper in a hat is feeling quite bold,
While squirrels gossip — oh, the tales they've told!

Tropical fruits hang low, oh so sweet,
But watch your heads, they might land at your feet.
The breeze laughs loudly as it whips around,
Tickling the flowers, having fun abound.

A crab in a shell gives an awkward wave,
He's the life of the party, so bright and brave.
With each little bump of an ailing bee,
The humor of nature is clear to see!

As night sets in with a twinkling grin,
Fireflies dance like they're wearing a pin.
Beneath the palms, silliness thrives,
In dreams of color, laughter derives.

The Lure of Fragrant Shadows

In shadows where aromas swirl and spin,
A monkey appears, grinning wide with his grin.
He steals a snack as if it's a game,
Making the blooms blush — oh, what a shame!

With petals fragrance that tickles the nose,
The flowers all gossip, as sweet scent flows.
A snail offers jokes without any shame,
As the wind adds laughter and whispers his name.

A wandering cat takes a misstep and slips,
Only to land in a pile of quips.
So join the ride on this fragrant thrill,
In the shadows of laughter, there's always a chill!

The blooms join in with a colorful cheer,
Every silly moment brings joy ever near.
In fragrant shadows, together we blend,
For laughter like this, you'll never want to end.

Midnight Rendezvous with Petals

The clock strikes twelve, and the flowers chime,
In a moonlit dance, they sway every time.
A raccoon in a tux steals the scene,
As petals twirl, feeling quite pristine!

Night creatures gather for a chat, oh so sly,
While fireflies twinkle, like stars in the sky.
A snail pulls a prank, sliming a shoe,
And giggles erupt in the midnight view.

Petals wear glimmers, reflecting bright light,
While frogs in top hats leap with delight.
Each drop of dew whispers, "Join in the fun!"
In this wild rendezvous, we are never done!

So here's to the midnight where laughter ignites,
Every petal a player in joyous flights.
In this charming world where silliness blooms,
The night sings sweetly, dispelling the glooms.

Sun-Kissed Blossoms at Dusk

Sunlit petals stretch and sway,
Dancing in a bright display.
Bees in bow ties laugh and twirl,
While butterflies begin to swirl.

Lemons laugh in shades of glee,
As ants hold hands for a spree.
Cacti wear their prickly hats,
Sipping tea with fancy brats.

Crickets sing a silly tune,
Underneath the crescent moon.
With every note, the flowers sway,
And giggle through the end of day.

A parrot jokes in borrowed rhymes,
While petals tease with silly chimes.
The night unfolds with laughter bright,
As blossoms wink and fade from sight.

The Garden of Forgotten Dreams

In a patch where wishes lay,
Dandelions play hide and sway.
Sleepy daisies yawn and stretch,
As rosemary jokes, 'Let's fetch!'

Worms wear top hats, digging deep,
While lilies nearly start to leap.
Forgotten dreams on leafy beds,
Share stories from their flower heads.

A tomato dreams of rolling hills,
While orchids plan to pay their bills.
Sunflowers think they're crowned in gold,
Whispering tales that never get old.

The wind joins in, a gentle tease,
Making flowers sway with ease.
In this garden, laughter grows,
Where even prickly thorns strike poses!

Nectar's Serenade

Hummingbirds in sequined suits,
Flitting by in joyful hoots.
Every flower, dressed to charm,
Offers sweetness with no harm.

Bees in sunglasses buzz about,
While pods giggle, there's no doubt.
Sun drops laughter from the sky,
As pals on petals all comply.

Mimosa shakes its sleepy head,
Tickled by a breeze instead.
Drunk on nectar, songs arise,
Roses join in, oh what a surprise!

Daisies sway to nature's beat,
While lilacs mingle in the heat.
Come join the garden's sweet parade,
Where everyone loves this serenade!

Colors of a Verdant Embrace

In greens and yellows, laughter flows,
Petals tickle as the wind blows.
A chorus of colors, wild and free,
Painting joy on every tree.

Orange poppies throw a party,
While violets play and get all hearty.
In this garden of wacky hues,
Marigolds sport their party shoes.

Cucumbers crack up with a smile,
Competing with radishes in style.
In this embrace of vibrant cheer,
Every blossom spreads good cheer.

Dancing shadows bounce and slide,
With hues that twist and turn with pride.
Join the fun, let laughter blend,
In this space where colors mend!

Castaways of the Isle in Bloom

We lounged on coconuts, feeling quite bright,
Twisting our limbs in pure daylight.
A parrot squawked, 'Get me a drink!'
We said, 'Just water, what do you think?'

With flowers aplenty, they danced in the breeze,
But tried to point out, 'You're doing this with ease!'
We chuckled and wiggled, what a sight to see,
When trees started laughing, even the sea!

We painted our faces with juice from the fruit,
The more we slipped, the sillier our loot.
A crab in a tuxedo joined our parade,
Claiming he'd always wanted to play charade!

So if you find us on this sandy shore,
With laughter and petals, you'll find us evermore.
Just know we are castaways, full of cheer,
With flowers as our hats, and cold drinks near!

Epiphanies Under the Canopy

Under branches where the sunshine plays,
We thought about life and its puzzling ways.
A squirrel appeared, with a nut on its head,
It looked like a hat, that darn nut had said!

We pondered so deeply, but what did we find?
An orange rose whispered, 'Life's really quite kind.'
Then a bee buzzed past, oh so yellow and bold,
Claiming, 'I'm here to make honey, not gold!'

But then came a monkey, swinging so free,
Yelling, 'I've found wisdom, come swing with me!'
With each little laugh, under the leafy expanse,
We figured out life is all about dance!

So if you're out hunting for pearls of deep thought,
Look to the blooms and the messes they brought.
In giggles and petals, life's truths were shown,
With laughter and ruckus, we felt not alone!

A Symphony of Color and Light

On an island stage where colors collide,
We danced with the daisies, with stars as our guide.
A juggler of lilies tossed blooms in the air,
While a laughing fern shouted, 'This show's beyond rare!'

With every bright petal, a note played so sweet,
A concert of hues made our hearts skip a beat.
The sun played the drums, a coconut gleamed,
As the audience clapped, everyone beamed!

A crab in a tutu declared, 'Encore!'
As the blooms raised their voices, wanting more.
'Let's paint the sky with our vibrant delight!'
So we painted and twirled till the fall of the night.

And just like that, under brilliant moonlight,
We found our pure joy in the colorful sight.
Each flower a note in our symphony loud,
With laughter and joy, we played to the crowd!

Flora that Dances in the Wind

In a garden where everything wiggles and sways,
The blossoms threw parties at all hours of days.
A daisy in polka dots winked with a grin,
'Come dance with us, let the fun times begin!'

With the breeze as our partner, we twirled around,
Swaying with giggles, our happiness found.
A bee did the cha-cha, while petals would twirl,
And a tulip tried breakdancing, what a whirl!

The hibiscus got dizzy, fell over in style,
We cheered as the sun threw down a broad smile.
'You folks are a riot!' said a sunflower large,
As it joined in the jig, and the world took charge.

So if you should wander where laughter's a draw,
Watch the blooms that dance without any flaw.
With petals and giggles, they've made quite a stand,
In a garden alive, under Sun's playful hand!

A Tapestry of Sun and Shade

In the garden, a parrot squawks,
Wearing a hat, he struts and talks.
Palm trees wave in a breezy dance,
Even the flowers are joining the prance.

Bumblebees buzz with a cheeky smile,
They sip on nectar, all the while.
Sunshine tickles each petal bright,
While lizards laugh in the fading light.

Coconuts drop with a thud and a crack,
Squirrels scurry, then playfully lack.
Mischief blooms like colorful buds,
As giggles tumble from grassy floods.

Beneath the shade, a picnic is set,
Ants in a line make the best of a bet.
Watermelon smiles, all juicy and neat,
What's summer without a bit of sweet?

Echoes of the Blossoming Isles

Giggling flowers sway with glee,
One says to another, 'Look at me!'
A hibiscus blushes, a rose rolls its eyes,
'We're the queens of the garden, no need for disguise.'

Butterflies glide in a fancy parade,
Matching their colors, all brightly displayed.
They tease a bee with a wobbly tease,
'Catch us if you can, oh little fuzz beast!'

Bananas hang low, sporting a grin,
Too yellow, they say, for an island's whim.
While mangoes chuckle, 'We're ripe for the pick!'
But only in salads – that's the real trick!

Coconuts giggle as they drop with a thud,
'You thought we were light? It's all just a dud!'
As laughter bursts through from root to the tip,
In this island escape, let your worries slip!

Enigma of the Vivid Canopy

Above, the leaves whisper secret jokes,
While vines tangle up like mischievous folks.
A gecko peers out with a knowing smirk,
He's the king, so they all do the work.

Frogs in tuxedos sing in a band,
With drumming beetles, oh so well-planned.
Each croak gets a laugh, a brilliant encore,
Who knew a swamp could hold such folklore?

Sunlight sprinkles like glittering spritz,
On cheeky chiquititas that just won't sit.
'We bloom for the party!' giggle the hues,
With petals that flirt in a breezy muse.

The canopy hides, yet encourages play,
As giggles and rustles sweep worries away.
Beneath the vast sky, so vibrant and wide,
Every creature joins in, let laughter abide.

Portrait of a Verdant Paradise

In a lush canvas, colors collide,
Petals prance forth, a jubilant ride.
Laughter erupts from the roses' bright cheer,
Their fragrance alone could bring folks near.

A snail in shades claims he's on a spree,
'Look at me zoom, oh so fast,' says he.
While daisies gossip about the hot sun,
'Who's stealing our spotlight? This just isn't fun!'

Cacti are stiff but crack a joke,
'We may seem prickly, but we can poke!'
As laughter pours like rain from a cloud,
In this wild bloom, they're wonderfully loud.

With each flutter, a spirit soars high,
Humor and color dance under the sky.
A celebration where petals can sing,
This garden of giggles is a marvelous thing!

Whispers of Exotic Petals

A parrot stole my picnic fare,
While bidding blooms a cheeky dare.
They giggle with a fragrance bold,
While ants march in a line of gold.

The orchids wore their colors bright,
And danced away without a fright.
A coconut dropped with a thud,
Mistaking head for a cozy bud.

The hibiscus winked with allure,
While bees buzzed 'round, they all adore.
"Take a seat on my soft leaf!"
Cried the garden, with glee and chief.

In shadows, snails host a parade,
While lizards think they're all so laid.
Oh, the joy in this green space,
Where petals giggle in a race.

Dance of the Lush Canopy

The leaves are shimmying to a tune,
While monkeys swing beneath the moon.
The mangoes drop, a juicy show,
As squirrels dance in a lively flow.

Palm fronds wave like they're in glee,
With shadows that hide a bumblebee.
The sunbeams play peekaboo,
As flowers sprout a funny hue.

A toucan spills its breakfast treat,
With seeds that roll beneath my feet.
I trip and land on a soft petal,
And laugh at nature's cheeky metal.

The breeze whispers jokes, oh so sly,
As butterflies wink and drift by.
In this vibrant scene, so spry,
Nature's laughter fills the sky.

Vibrant Hues of Paradise

In colors bold, the lilies boast,
As daisies prepare for a garden roast.
A bee wore stripes, but looked like a clown,
Buzzing about in its funny gown.

The petals burst with a giggly force,
While frogs joined in, a jumping course.
"What color am I?" a flower quipped,
As a passerby strolled, a smile heipped.

With colors that might always clash,
The roses blushed and made a splash.
They held a party, but quite absurd,
Inviting all, except for the bird!

Sunsets draped their canvas wide,
While shadows danced in laughter's stride.
In this garden, vibrant and free,
Nature's comedy is the key.

Secrets Woven in Fragrance

A secret whispered from a vine,
As daisies plotted under the pine.
They laughed about the sun's warm touch,
While snails gossip in a leafy clutch.

Neath pandan leaves, a riddle spun,
'Why did the flower never run?'
The answer flew with a bumble cheer,
'Because it blooms right here, my dear!'

The jasmine curled, its scent a tease,
As frogs joined in, laughing with ease.
They shared tales of a daring sprout,
With petals that danced and never pout.

A lizard claimed, with utmost pride,
That he could glide with the best outside.
In a garden filled with glee and surprise,
The fragrance and laughter surely rise.

Serenity in the Orchard

In a grove where lemons dance,
A monkey steals a glance.
He's trying to make a joke,
But ends up perched on a bloke.

Cherries chuckle, ripe and red,
While peaches roll, avoiding bread.
A parrot sings a silly tune,
It's louder than a howling loon.

The apple trees plot a game,
To make the pears feel quite the same.
A bee buzzes with a grin,
As if it just won first place in a spin.

Limes are plotting a fruit parade,
Citrus voices, quite unafraid.
In laughter, they sway to and fro,
As humor ripes in sun's warm glow.

Melodies of Nature's Palette

On the canvas, colors splash,
A pineapple causes quite a clash.
It wears sunglasses, thinks it's cool,
While coconuts play hopscotch by the pool.

The violets who sing off-key,
Invite daisies for cup of tea.
They spill the brew; it paints the ground,
With laughter that's blissfully all around.

Hibiscus hats, they steal the show,
As tulips tango, toe to toe.
The breeze whispers jokes, soft and light,
As fireflies dance into the night.

Each hue has a quirk, it seems,
With laughter joining in their dreams.
Nature's palette plays the best,
In this garden jest, they are blessed.

Ascent of the Orchid

An orchid in a pot thinks it's grand,
With petals spread like a marching band.
It tries to sway but tips too far,
Lands on a sheet of chocolate tar.

Its neighbor, a cactus, rolls its eyes,
Saying, "No thorns, just silly lies!"
Yet they get along, a prickly pair,
Trading jokes while combing hair.

A bud arrives with much great hype,
It tells a tale of slippery type.
With roots in knots, they all agree,
This garden holds a mystery.

They giggle as the day turns dim,
In silliness, they find their whim.
For life is not forced to be bland,
With laughter and fun at their command.

Colors of the Evening Sky

The sun dips low, what a sight,
Clouds bathed in hues of peachy light.
A seagull jokes, 'This is too much,'
While crabs applaud with oceans' touch.

With giggles, orange bursts begin,
As purple grapes roll down the skin.
The stars poke fun, all twinkly bright,
At galaxies dressed for the night.

The horizon flirts, a playful tease,
While breezes carry whispers of ease.
Fireflies blink in comic poses,
Trailing laughter among the roses.

As evening chuckles and takes a bow,
The colors laugh, "We'll show you how!"
In nature's jest, the world unwinds,
A playful canvas, joy it finds.

www.ingramcontent.com/pod-product-compliance
Lightning Source LLC
Chambersburg PA
CBHW060119230426
43661CB00003B/254